Pebble®
Plus

Snakes

Rattlesnakes

by Mary R. Dunn

Consultants:
Christopher E. Smith, M.Sc., A.W.B.
President, Minnesota Herpetological Society
Gail Saunders-Smith, PhD,
consulting editor

CAPSTONE PRESS
a capstone imprint

Pebble Plus is published by Capstone Press,
1710 Roe Crest Drive, North Mankato, Minnesota 56003.
www.capstonepub.com

Library of Congress Cataloging-in-Publication Data
Dunn, Mary R.
Rattlesnakes / by Mary Dunn.
p. cm.—(Pebble plus. Snakes)
Summary: "Simple text and full-color photographs describe rattlesnakes"—Provided by publisher.
Audience: 005-008.
Audience: K to grade 3.
Includes bibliographical references and index.
ISBN 978-1-4765-2085-8 (library binding)
ISBN 978-1-4765-3486-2 (eBook PDF)
1. Rattlesnakes—Juvenile literature. I. Title.
QL666.O69D864 2014
597.96'38—dc23   2013007430

Editorial Credits
Jeni Wittrock, editor; Kyle Grenz, designer; Eric Manske, production specialist

Photo Credits
Alamy: Bill Gorum, 15; Corbis: imagebroker/Rolf Nussbaumer, 9, Joe McDonald, 11, Visuals Unlimited/Jack Milchanowski, 21; National Geographic Stock: Joel Sartore, 5; Science Source: John Serrao, 17, Tom McHugh, 13, 19; Shutterstock: Heiko Kiera, 1, Jason Mintzer, cover, Matt Jeppson, 7, vlastas66, design element (throughout)

Note to Parents and Teachers

The Snakes set supports national science standards related to biology and life science. This book describes and illustrates rattlesnakes. The images support early readers in understanding the text. The repetition of words and phrases helps early readers learn new words. This book also introduces early readers to subject-specific vocabulary words, which are defined in the Glossary section. Early readers may need assistance to read some words and to use the Table of Contents, Glossary, Read More, Internet Sites, and Index sections of the book.

Printed in the United States of America in North Mankato, Minnesota.
032013   007223CGF13.

Table of Contents

Rattling Reptile

Rattle, rattle, rattle!
Rattlesnakes are known for
their rattling sound. It comes
from hard skin shaped like
buttons on their tails.

5

About 30 kinds of rattlesnakes live in North and South America. They make their homes in deserts, swamps, forests, and grasslands.

Rattlesnake Range

☐ where rattlesnakes live

North America

Europe

Asia

Africa

South America

Australia

Antarctica

N W E S

Rattlesnake Bodies

Rattlesnakes' bodies can be gray, yellow, rust, or black. They have dark markings on their scales.

A rattlesnake has small
organs called pits. The pits
sense the heat of nearby prey.
Pits help a rattler find
prey, even in the dark.

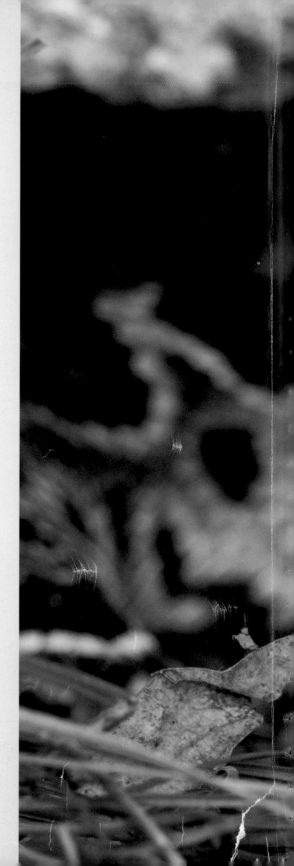

Mealtime

A rattlesnake has a dangerous bite. Its fangs sink into its prey. Venom in the fangs quickly kills the prey. The snake swallows its meal.

Rattlesnakes hunt mice,
birds, rabbits, and other
small animals. Young rattlers
eat about once a week.
Older rattlers eat less often.

Growing Up

Female rattlesnakes have 10 to 20 babies at time. Young snakes leave their mothers after a few weeks.

Before winter, young rattlers
follow their mother's scent.
They hibernate in her den.
In the wild, rattlesnakes
can live about 25 years.

In Danger

Many hunters kill rattlesnakes for their skins. They use skins to make belts and boots. In some places, there are laws to protect rattlesnakes.

Glossary

den—a place where an animal lives

fang—a long, sharp, pointed tooth

hibernate—to spend winter in a deep sleep

pit—a small hole near a snake's eyes that senses warm animals

prey—an animal that is hunted by another animal for food

scale—one of many small, hard pieces of skin that cover an animal's body

scent—a smell

venom—a liquid poison made by an animal to kill its prey

Read More

Gunderson, Megan M. *Diamondback Rattlesnakes.* Snakes. Edina, Minn.: ABDO Pub. Co., 2011.

Macken, JoAnn Early. *Rattlesnakes.* Animals that Live in the Desert. Pleasantville, N.Y.: Weekly Reader, 2010.

Sexton, Colleen. *Rattlesnakes.* Snakes Alive! Minneapolis: Bellwether Media, 2010.

Internet Sites

FactHound offers a safe, fun way to find Internet sites related to this book. All of the sites on FactHound have been researched by our staff.

Here's all you do:

Visit *www.facthound.com*

Type in this code: 9781476520858

Index

Word Count: 193
Grade: 1
Early-Intervention Level: 18